MEDITATIONS ON LIFE ~ DEATH

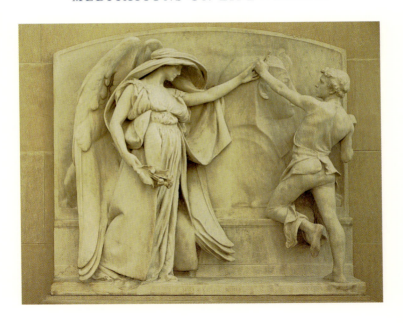

Voces Novae

VOCES NOVAE

Voces Novae was founded in 1996 to create programs that would enrich and inform how we live. We wanted to use the arts to cut through what Virginia Woolfe called "the cotton-wool of daily life," to achieve wide-awakeness and experience most fully what it means to be human. "Meditations on Life ~ Death" assembles music and literature representing the human struggle with mortality. Mortality, as many poets suggest, may be the defining quality of the human condition; yet we live in a culture that regards death as a medical event, stripped of its meaning, its grace, and its grandeur. Hospice organizations are working to change the culture of death and dying, placing more emphasis on its emotional and spiritual dimensions. "Meditations" is based on the belief that the contemplation of one's own mortality is a valuable part of life, that it enhances our experience of consciousness and gives meaning to the present moment. It is not intended as anesthesia or an escape. It is intended, rather, as an opportunity for engagement with ideas and aesthetics. It is for those who find peace and comfort in contemplating the marvelous.

Project Origins

In September of 1986, the Reverend Larry Hill, conductor and founder of the Back Bay Chorale in Boston and its sister organization, the Pro Arte Chamber Orchestra, announced in rehearsal one evening that Michelle, principal flautist of the orchestra, was dying of cancer. She was thirty years old. That night, the Chorale recorded some hymns for Michelle. Larry Hill then arranged for some of Michelle's friends to read to her, and together with a recording of the Brahms *Requiem* which the orchestra and chorus had recently made, he assembled tapes for her to listen to each night. She died a few weeks later.

Ever since, I have wanted to combine music with readings to provide comfort to those facing death. My conviction was made stronger by the fact that Larry Hill himself died unexpectedly of cancer within a few months of caring for Michelle. This recording, then, is a tribute to the legacy of Larry Hill, and it is his voice you hear speaking the invocation at the opening of each meditation, an invocation he originally recorded for Michelle.

The cornerstone of this project is Bach's *Cantata No. 106*, whose structure suggests an emotional journey through a series of themes: God's Time; Put Your House in Order; Death's Inevitability; Acceptance; Paradise; and Transcendence. "Meditations" borrows this structure for its cycle of choral works and readings. An opening movement is added, entitled "Music as Solace," which explores music's role as comforter and spiritual catalyst. That section begins with John Wilbye's *Draw on, sweet night*, an earthbound plea for solace. With an air of self-pity —"draw on, sweet night, best time for my complaining"— Wilbye's work provides a starting point in the process of coming to terms with impending death. Edna St. Vincent Millay's poem, *On Listening to a Symphony of Beethoven*, provides a response. In her poem, music is a source of solace, "my rampart, and my only one." Elliot Carter's *To Music* also shows us how music may ease the journey from illness to peace to death.

The second meditation, "God's Time," celebrates the divinity of the moment, sensual pleasures, and the fullness of life. *i thank You God for most this amazing* by E.E. Cummings begins the meditation. Wallace Stevens'

Sunday Morning questions the distinctions between life and the hereafter and emphasizes the divinity of the here and now. *That Time of Year* by Shakespeare hints that the "here and now" is limited. Our time is short.

The third meditation, "Put Your House in Order," continues to explore earthbound themes. George Eliot's commentary acknowledges that the "first pangs" of awareness cannot be avoided. References throughout the Eliot commentary and Edward Elgar's *How Calmly the Evening* suggest the importance of human relations and caring at this critical point in life.

The fourth meditation, "Death's Inevitability," begins the process of moving beyond. Emily Dickinson's *I Heard a Fly Buzz* depicts the actual moment of death. Then comes transcendence in the voice of Walt Whitman, "Darest thou, O soul, walk out with me toward the unknown region?" a challenge to experience death wide awake.

The fifth meditation, "Acceptance," begins with a plea for rest in Calvin Hampton's *O Lord, Support Us*. It is followed by Robert Frost's *Acceptance*, a nature poem about the setting sun, which welcomes darkness with feelings of comfort and trust in "what will be." A.E. Houseman's *Parta Quies* grants permission to let go, and the meditation ends with the familiar equation of death with sleep.

The sixth meditation, "Paradise," brings visions of ever-increasing beauty as the angelic hierarchy is ascended in William Harris' *Faire is the Heaven*. Rilke's *Duino Elegy No. I* fuses life and death, encompassing the whole of human experience at once and suggesting that music had its origin in mourning death. Donald Martino's *Eternitie*, based on a poem by Robert Herrick, presents a vision of timelessness and infinity in which "yeares and age" are "drowned in one endlesse day." Herrick's vision draws comfort through imaginative and philosophical exploration, a significant advance over the temporary relief sought in *Draw on, sweet night*, which began the "Meditations" cycle.

The Sleep, by Elizabeth Barrett Browning, opens the final meditation. The Bach cantata then provides a glorious coda, a recapitulation of the journey.

While the cycle began with night, it ends with day. While it began with earthly complaint, it ends with eternal peace. We encourage your exploration of the interconnections between the various poems, readings, visual images and musical works that make up "Meditations."

Voces Novae is an amateur choir that rehearses once a week. We compiled this project as a way of examining our own ideas about death, with the hope that the wisdom of these words and music will be of use and comfort to others as well. We consulted no focus groups, we hired no ringers, and we sought not to over-produce the recordings in an effort to keep them immediate and human. This recording and book are simply a gift from the heart of everyone involved, to all, to each.

—Aaron Kercheval

NOTES ON MUSIC

The works in this compilation reflect the belief that composers, poets, and artists offer more than escape from life's experiences and tribulations, that they are the hand that points to something beyond —something richer, more deeply felt and more complex, something divine. Some of the music is soothing and pretty, such as the Barber, the Elgar, the Gawthrop, the Welsh hymn —but some of it is also knotty and intense. Elliott Carter's setting of the Herrick poem *To Musique, to Becalme His Fever* fairly reels with the pain of fever, the narrator pleading for music to provide relief, until the dissonances resolve at the end into a blissful unison.

The combination of William Schuman's music with Walt Whitman's remarkable poetry is especially potent. Here, too, the unison is used to great effect. In *The Last Invocation*, many phrases begin with the choir all on the same note, and then they pull apart —reluctantly, by small, dissonant steps. In the last phrase of the piece, "Strong is your hold, O love," Schuman widens the singers' range, increasing the intensity, until on the final "O love," the upper three voices sing a consonant triad, while the bass sings a dissonant note. We believe that bass note represents everything we love down here in this messy world, everything that makes it hard to let go.

In *The Unknown Region*, Schuman sets Whitman's challenge, "Darest thou now" as a whispering canon. It nips at the edges of our consciousness until it grows, with a great crescendo, to the great confrontation —the direct address to the soul: "Darest thou now, O soul, walk out with me to the unknown region?" The line, "I know it not, O soul. Nor dost thou. All is a blank before us in that region" is set twice: first as an inversion of the canon which opens the piece. The second statement returns to the hesitant "walk out" of *The Last Invocation* —beginning on octave A's and gradually stepping apart until "All waits, undream'd of in that region, that inaccessible land," where we are suspended in a kind of exquisite limbo before moving firmly and inexorably into the final cadence.

After the opening invocation of *To All, To Each*, Schuman has the sopranos, second tenors and basses spin a haunting, undulating melody in thirds, while at the center of the texture, the altos and first tenors sing a pedal tone, an E that is not insistent but never wavers. It is the perfect realization of Whitman's text, "To all, to each, sooner or later, delicate death." The Carter and the Schuman pieces are certainly the most dissonant works in this compilation —their portrayal of pain, resistance, and struggle are very real. Even the exquisite *Draw on, sweet night* has a few pungent cross-relations, which set off the plaintive quality of the text. At the other end of the emotional scale are the visions of angels and paradise portrayed in Harris' *Faire is the Heaven*, in which two choirs take turns extolling the glories to come in beautiful Anglican harmonies. William Billings' *Washington* portrays a rollicking chariot ride, and the musical imagery of Donald Martino's *Eternitie* is similar to the textual imagery of *Faire is the Heaven* —the voice parts often enter one after the other, climbing higher and higher.

The meditative cycle is defined by the Bach, which ends and summarizes the emotional journey. From the dignified opening Sinfonia to the ecstatic final "amen," Bach provides music that is dense and satisfying.

The central chorus provides a stunning musical interpretation of the crux of the matter: we must die, we welcome death. The opening of the movement, an old testament text ("It is the old covenant, you must die") is composed in the severe style of Bach's ancestors, spinning out in accordance with established compositional rules; but when the sopranos enter with a melody full of confidence and joy ("Yea, come, Lord Jesus!"), their last passionate outburst leaves us hanging, breathless.

—Susan Swaney

Claude Monet, *Morning on the Seine Near Giverny*, 1897

Samuel Palmer, *Moonrise*

MUSIC AS SOLACE

Oh God, grant us a peaceful evening, a calm night, and a perfect end.

Draw on, sweet night

by John Wilbye

Draw on, sweet night, best friend unto those cares,
That do arise from painful melancholy.
My life so ill through want of comfort fares,
That unto thee, I consecrate it wholly.
Sweet night draw on.
My griefs when they be told
To shades and darkness, find some ease from paining.
And while thou all in silence dost enfold,
I then shall have best time for my complaining.

Fernand Khnopff, *Listening to Schumann*, 1883

On Hearing a Symphony of Beethoven

Sweet sounds, oh, beautiful music, do not cease!
Reject me not into the world again.
With you alone is excellence and peace,
Mankind made plausible, his purpose plain.
Enchanted in your air benign and shrewd,
With limbs asprawl and empty faces pale,
The spiteful and the stingy and the rude
Sleep like scullions in the fairy tale.
This moment is the best the world can give:
The tranquil blossom on the tortured stem.
Reject me not, sweet sounds! Oh, let me live,
Till doom espy my towers and scatter them,
A city spellbound under the aging sun,
Music my rampart, and my only one.

—Edna St. Vincent Millay

To Music

by Elliott Carter

(text by Robert Herrick —

To Musique, to Becalme His Fever—1648)

Charm me asleep, and melt me so
With thy delicious numbers;
That being ravisht, hence I goe
Away in easie slumbers.
Ease my sick head,
And make my bed,
Thou Power, that canst sever
From me this ill:
And quickly still:
Though thou not kill
My Fever.

Thou sweetly canst convert the same
From a consuming fire,
Into a gentle licking flame,
And make it thus expire.
Then make me weep
My paines asleep;
And give me such reposes,
That I, poore I,
May think, thereby,
I live and die
'Mongst roses.

Fall on me like a silent dew,
Or like those Maiden showers,
Which, by the peepe of day, doe strew
A Baptime o'er the flowers.
Melt, melt my paines,
With thy soft strains;
That having ease me given,
With full delight,
I leave this light;
And take my flight
For Heaven.

Sarabande

by William Croft

Henri Matisse, *Ivy Branch*, 1941

II

GOD'S TIME

❦

Oh God, grant us a peaceful evening, a calm night, and a perfect end.

Happy Air

by Mussard

In eternity there is indeed something true and sublime.
But all these times and places and occasions are now and here.
God himself culminates in the present moment,
and will never be more divine in the lapse of all the ages.

—Thoreau, *Walden*

Simple Pastimes

by Mussard

Pierre Bonnard, *The Open Window*, 1921

i thank You God for most this amazing

i thank You God for most this amazing
day: for leaping greenly spirits of trees
and a blue true dream of sky; and for everything
which is natural which is infinite which is yes

(i who have died am alive again today,
and this is the sun's birthday; this is the birth
day of life and of love and wings; and of the gay
great happening illimitably earth)

how should tasting touching hearing seeing
breathing any — lifted from the no
of all nothing — human merely being
doubt unimaginable You?

(now the ears of my ears awake and
now the eyes of my eyes are opened)

—E. E. Cummings

Crowns of Sweet Roses
by G.F. Handel

Sunday Morning

Complacencies of the peignoir, and late
Coffee and oranges in a sunny chair,
And the green freedom of a cockatoo
Upon a rug mingle to dissipate
The holy hush of ancient sacrifice.
She dreams a little, and she feels the dark
Encroachment of that old catastrophe,
As a calm darkens among water lights.
The pungent oranges and bright, green wings
Seem things in some procession of the dead,
Winding across wide water, without sound.
The day is like wide water, without sound,
Stilled for the passing of her dreaming feet
Over the seas, to silent Palestine,
Dominion of the blood and sepulcher.

Why should she give her bounty to the dead?
What is divinity if it can come
Only in silent shadows and in dreams?
Shall she not find in comforts of the sun,
In pungent fruit and bright, green wings, or else
In any balm or beauty of the earth,
Things to be cherished like the thought of heaven?
Divinity must live within herself:
Passions of rain, or moods in falling snow;
Grievings in loneliness, or unsubdued
Elations when the forest blooms; gutsy
Emotions on wet roads on autumn nights;
All pleasures and all pains, remembering
The bough of summer and the winter branch.
These are the measures destined for her soul.

Jove in the clouds had his inhuman birth.
No mother suckled him, no sweet land gave
Large-mannered motions to his mythy mind.

He moved among us, as a muttering king,
Magnificent, would move among his hinds,
Until our blood, commingling, virginal,
With heaven, brought such requital to desire
The very hinds discerned it, in a star.
Shall our blood fail? Or shall it come to be
The blood of paradise? And shall the earth
Seem all of paradise that we shall know?
The sky will be much friendlier then than now,
A part of labor and a part of pain,
And next in glory to enduring love,
Not this dividing and indifferent blue.

She says, "I am content when wakened birds,
Before they fly, test the reality
Of misty fields, by their sweet questionings;
But when the birds are gone, and their warm fields
Return no more, where, then, is paradise?"
There is not any haunt of prophecy,

Nor any old chimera of the grave,
Neither the golden underground, nor isle
Melodious, where spirits gat them home,
Nor visionary south, nor cloudy palm
Remote on heaven's hill, that has endured
As April's green endures; or will endure
Like her remembrance of awakened birds,
Or her desire for June and evening, tipped
By the consummation of the swallow's wings.

She says, "But in contentment I still feel
The need of some imperishable bliss."
Death is the mother of beauty; hence from her,
Alone, shall come fulfillment to our dreams
And our desires. Although she strews the leaves
Of sure obliteration on our paths,
The path sick sorrow took, the many paths
Where triumph rang its brassy phrase, or love
Whispered a little out of tenderness,

She makes the willow shiver in the sun
For maidens who were wont to sit and gaze
Upon the grass, relinquished to their feet.
She causes boys to pile new plums and pears
On disregarded plate. The maidens taste
And stray impassioned in the littering leaves.

Is there no change of death in paradise?
Does ripe fruit never fall? Or do the boughs
Hang always heavy in that perfect sky,
Unchanging, yet so like our perishing earth,
With rivers like our own that seek for seas
They never find, the same receding shores
That never touch with inarticulate pang?
Why set the pear upon those riverbanks
Or spice the shores with odors of the plum?
Alas, that they should wear our colors there,
The silken weavings of our afternoons,
And pick the strings of our insipid lutes!

Death is the mother of beauty, mystical,
Within whose burning bosom we devise
Our earthly mothers waiting, sleeplessly.

Supple and turbulent, a ring of men
Shall chant in orgy on a summer morn
Their boisterous devotion to the sun,
Not as a god, but as a god might be,
Naked among them, like a savage source.
Their chant shall be a chant of paradise,
Out of their blood, returning to the sky;
And in their chant shall enter, voice by voice,
The windy lake wherein their lord delights,
The trees, like seraphim, and echoing hills,
That choir among themselves long afterward.
They shall know well the heavenly fellowship
Of men that perish and of summer morn.
And whence they came and whither they shall go
The dew upon their feet shall manifest.

She hears, upon that water without sound,
A voice that cries, "The tomb in Palestine
Is not the porch of spirits lingering.
It is the grave of Jesus, where he lay."
We live in an old chaos of the sun,
Or old dependency of day and night,
Or island solitude, unsponsored, free,
Of that wide water, inescapable.
Deer walk upon our mountains, and the quail
Whistle about us their spontaneous cries;
Sweet berries ripen in the wilderness;
And, in the isolation of the sky,
At evening, casual flocks of pigeons make
Ambiguous undulations as they sink,
Downward to darkness, on extended wings.

—Wallace Stevens

John Singer Sargent, *Pomegranates*, 1908

Sure on This Shining Night

by Samuel Barber

(text by James Agee from *Permit Me Voyage*)

Sure on this shining night
Of star-made shadows round,
Kindness must watch for me
This side the ground.
The late year lies down the north.
All is healed, all is health.
High summer holds earth.
Hearts all whole.
Sure on this shining night
I weep for wonder wand'ring far alone
Of shadows on the stars.
On this shining night.

That Time of Year

That time of year thou mayst in me behold
When yellow leaves, or none, or few, do hang
Upon those boughs which shake against the cold,
Bare ruined choirs where late the sweet birds sang.
In me thou see'st the twilight of such day
As after sunset fadeth in the west,
Which by and by black night doth take away,
Death's second self, that seals up all in rest.
In me thou see'st the glowing of such fire,
That on the ashes of his youth doth lie
As the deathbed whereon it must expire,
Consumed with that which it was nourished by.
    This thou perceivest, which makes thy love more strong,
    To love that well which thou must leave ere long.

—William Shakespeare

Close Now Thine Eyes

by Daniel E. Gawthrop

(text by Francis Quarles)

Close now thine eyes and rest secure:
Thy *Soule* is safe enough; thy *Body* sure;
He that loves thee, He that keeps
and guards thee, never slumbers, never sleepes.
The smiling Conscience in a sleeping breast
Has only peace, has only rest:
The musicke and the mirth of Kings,
Are all but very *Discordes*, when she sings:
Then close thine eyes and rest secure;
No sleepe so sweet as thine, no rest so sure.

Pupil of Rembrandt Harmensz van Rijn, *Old Man in Prayer*

III

PUT YOUR HOUSE IN ORDER

Oh God, grant us a peaceful evening, a calm night, and a perfect end.

How Calmly the Evening
by Edward Elgar
(text by T. T. Lynch)

How calmly the evening once more is descending,
As kind as a promise, as still as a prayer;
O wing of the Lord, in Thy shelter befriending,
May we and our households continue to share.

We come to be soothed with Thy merciful healing;
The dews of the night cure the wounds of the day;
We come, our life's work and its brevity feeling,
With thanks for the past, for the future we pray.

Lord, save us from folly; be with us in sorrow;
Sustain us in work till the time of our rest;
When earth's day is over, may heaven's tomorrow
Dawn on us, of homes long expected possest.

For the first sharp pangs there is no comfort; whatever goodness may surround us, darkness and silence still hang about our pain. But slowly, the clinging companionship with the dead is linked with our living affections and duties, and we begin to feel our sorrow as a solemn initiation, preparing us for that sense of loving, pitying fellowship with the fullest human lot, which, I must think no one who has tasted it will deny to be the chief blessedness of our life. And especially to know what the last parting is seems needful to give the utmost sanctity of tenderness to our relations with each other …. All the experience that makes my communion with your grief is summed up in a "God bless you," which represents the swelling of my heart now, as I write, thinking of you and your sense of what has been and is not.

—George Eliot

Suite in G Major - Sarabande

by Marin Marais

What wouldst thou be found doing when overtaken by Death? If I might choose, I would be found doing some deed of true humanity, of wide import, beneficent and noble. But if I may not be found engaged in aught so lofty, let me hope at least for this —what none may hinder, what is surely in my power— that I may be found raising up in myself that which had fallen; learning to deal more wisely with the things of sense; working out my own tranquillity, and thus rendering that which is its due to every relation of life …

If death surprise me thus employed, it is enough if I can stretch forth my hands to God and say, "The faculties which I received at Thy hands for apprehending this thine Administration, I have not neglected. As far as in me lay, I have done Thee no dishonour. Behold how I have used the senses, the primary conceptions which Thou gavest me. Have I ever laid anything to Thy charge? Have I ever murmured at aught that came to pass, or wished it otherwise? Have I in anything transgressed the relations of life? For that Thou didst beget me, I thank Thee for that Thou has given: for the time during which I have used the things that were Thine, it suffices me. Take them back and place them whereever Thou wilt! They were all Thine, and Thou gavest them me.: — If a man depart thus minded, is it not enough? What life is fairer or more noble, what end happier than this? —Epictetus

God that madest earth and heaven

God, that madest earth and heaven,
Darkness and light;
Who the day for toil has given,
For rest the night;
May Thine angel guards defend us,
Slumber sweet Thy mercy send us;
Holy dreams and hopes attend us,
This live long night.

And when morn again shall call us
To run life's way,
May we still, whate'er befall us,
Thy will obey.
From the power of evil hide us,
In the narrow pathway guide us,
Nor Thy smile be e'er denied us
The live long day.

Guard us waking, guard us sleeping,
And when we die,
May we in Thy mighty keeping
All peaceful lie;
When the last dread call shall wake us,
Do not Thou, our God, forsake us,
But to reign in glory take us
With Thee on high.

Vincent van Gogh, *The Starry Night*, 1889

IV

INEVITABLE DEATH

Oh God, grant us a peaceful evening, a calm night, and a perfect end.

Creator of the Stars of Night

Creator of the stars of night,
Your people's everlasting light,
O God, deliverer of us all,
We pray Thee hear us when we call.

When this old world drew on toward night,
Thou gave us stars in splendor bright.
The sun shines as creation sleeps.
Grant us the gift of sleep that's deep.

John McCrady, *Swing Low, Sweet Chariot,* 1937

I Heard a Fly Buzz When I Died

I heard a fly buzz—when I died—
The Stillness in the Room
Was like the Stillness in the Air—
Between the Heaves of Storm—

The Eyes—around had wrung them dry—
And Breaths were gathering firm
For that last Onset—when the King
Be witnessed—in the Room—

I willed my Keepsakes—Signed away
What portion of me be
Assignable—and then it was
There interposed a Fly—

With Blue—uncertain stumbling Buzz—
Between the light—and me—
And then the Windows failed—and then
I could not see to see—

—Emily Dickinson

Mark Rothko, *Untitled*, 1969

Carols of Death

by William Schuman
(text by Walt Whitman)

The Last Invocation

At the last, tenderly,
From the walls of the powerful fortress'd house,
From the clasp of the knitted locks, from the keep of the
well closed doors,
Let me be wafted.
Let me glide noiselessly forth;
With the key of softness unlock the locks with a whisper,
Set ope the doors, O soul.
Tenderly! be not impatient!
Strong is your hold O mortal flesh,
Strong is your hold O love.

The Unknown Region

Darest thou now, O soul,
Walk out with me toward the unknown region,
Where neither ground is for the feet nor any path to follow?
No map there, no guide,
Nor voice sounding, nor touch of human hand,
Nor face with blooming flesh, nor lips, nor eyes, are in that land.
I know it not, O soul, all is a blank before us,
All waits undream'd of in that region, that inaccessible land.
The unknown region.

To All, To Each

Come lovely and soothing death,
Undulate round the world, serenely arriving,
In the day, in the night,
to all, to each,
Sooner or later delicate death.

Albert Pinkham Ryder, *Dead Bird*, 1890's

V

ACCEPTANCE

Oh God, grant us a peaceful evening, a calm night, and a perfect end.

O Lord, Support Us

by Calvin Hampton

(text from *The Book of Common Prayer*)

O Lord, support us all the day long, until the shadows lengthen and the
evening comes, and the busy world is hushed, and the fever of life is
over, and our work is done. O Lord, support us all the day long;
then in thy mercy grant us safe lodging,
and a holy rest and peace at last.
O Lord, support us all the day long. Amen.

Acceptance

When the spent sun throws up its rays on cloud
And goes down burning into the gulf below,
No voice in nature is heard to cry aloud
At what has happened. Birds, at least, must know
It is the change to darkness in the sky.
Murmuring something quiet in her breast,
One bird begins to close a faded eye;
Or overtaken too far from his nest,
Hurrying low above the grove, some waif
Swoops just in time to his remembered tree.
At most he thinks or twitters softly, "Safe!
Now let the night be dark for all of me.
Let the night be too dark for me to see
Into the future. Let what will be, be."

—Robert Frost

e flat Intermezzo

by Johannes Brahms

Parta Quies

Goodnight; ensured release,
Imperishable peace,
Have these for yours,
While sea abides, and land,
And earth's foundations stand,
And heaven endures.

When earth's foundations flee,
Nor sky nor land nor sea
At all is found,
Content you, let them burn:
It is not your concern;
Sleep on, sleep sound.

—A. E. Houseman

Death and Sleep

by Joseph Haydn

Death is a longer sleep,
Sleep is a shorter, shorter death,
And sleep can soothe,
but death dispels life's fretful cares.
Death is a longer sleep.

Calyx-krater, *Sleep and Death transporting the body of Sarpedon to Lycia, ca. 515 B.C.*

Pablo Picasso, *Evocation*, 1901

VI
PARADISE

Oh God, grant us a peaceful evening, a calm night, and a perfect end.

Washington

by William Billings

Lord, when thou dids't ascend on high,
Ten thousand angels fill'd the sky,
Ten thousand angels fill'd the sky;
Those heav'nly guards around thee wait,
Like chariots that attend thy state.

Thomas Cole, *Voyage of Life: Old Age*, 1840

Duino Elegy No. 1

Who, if I cried, would hear me among the angelic orders? And even if one of them took me suddenly to his heart, I should be absorbed utterly in his stronger being. For Beauty is only the dawn of a terror that we still are just able to bear, and which we adore because it serenely disdains to destroy us. Each angel is terrible. And so I restrain myself and stifle the heart-cry of desperate sobbing. Alas, who is there will come to help us? Not angels, not men, and the clever beasts are already aware that we do not feel too securely at home in this interpreted world. There remains, perhaps, some tree on a slope we daily see again; there remains for us yesterday's pathway and the clinging constancy of an old habit that like us, and lingered, and never left us. O, and the Night, the Night, when wind from the world-space bites our faces—, for whom would she not stay, the longed for, mild, disillusioning Night. To which of the lonely hearts is she painfully imminent? Is she kinder to lovers? Alas, they only conceal their lot with each other. Do you not know yet? Fling the emptiness from your arms into the spaces where we breathe—, the birds, perhaps, will feel the expanding air in quickened flight.

Yes, the Spring had need of you. Many a star beckoned for you to perceive it. Many a wave would lift toward you from the long ago, or else, perhaps a violin was sounding as you passed by an open window. All this was a portent. But did you comprehend it? Were you not always distracted by expectation —as though all this foretold a loved one? (Where will you keep hidden all the amazing, strange thoughts of her coming and going, often remaining through the night?) But when overcome by longing, sing the great lovers; not yet is their fame sufficiently immortalized. Those whom you almost envied, the forsaken, you found so much more lovable than those whose longing was gratified. Begin ever anew their never adequate praise: Think: how the Hero endures, even his downfall was only a plea for existence, his ultimate birth. But lovers are taken by exhausted Nature back to herself again, as though such creative force could not twice be exerted. Have you thought of Gaspara Stampa?

Any maiden, who had forever lost her lover, could feel from that far more intense example of loving; "If only I could become as she was!" Should not all of our old unending sufferings be yielding fruit by now? Is it not time, in loving, to free ourselves from the loved one and quivering endure: as the arrow endures the bow-string, to become, in the gathering outleap, something more than itself? For nothing is fixed forever.

Voices, voices, hear, my heart, as once, only the Holy heard: till the resounding call lifted them from the earth: but they still remained kneeling undistracted and undisturbed in their attention so intensely they listened. Not that you could endure the voice of God; far from it. But hark to the sighing, the uninterrupted tidings growing out of the silence, drifting now to you from those youthfully dead. Whenever you entered a church in Rome or in Naples was not their fate always quietly speaking to you? Or else an inscription gloriously impressed you, as recently, the tablet in Santa Maria Formosa. What do they wish of me? I must remove gently the semblance of suffered injustice, that hinds a little, at times, the pure adventure of the spirit.

How strange it is to live on the earth no longer, to use no longer the customs that we have acquired. Roses, and other things that for us are tokens of promise not to interpret in them the pledges of man's future; to be no longer all that we once were, all we have achieved with hands

47

endlessly anxious; to lay aside even one's own name like a broken plaything. Strange not to wish—not to continue wishing. Strange to see all that was once in relation, loosely fluttering in space. To be dead is difficult and full of incompletion before one is conscious of even a trace of eternity. —But the living make the mistake of drawing too sharp distinctions. Angels (it is said) are unaware often whether they move among the living or dead. The eternal torrent sweeps all the ages on through both realms, and sounds above both forever.

Finally they need us no more, the early-departed, one outgrows earthly things as one is gently weaned from the breasts of a mother. But we that have need of such mighty secrets,—we, for whom grief is so often the source of blessed progress—; could we exist without them? Is the legend in vain, how once, mourning for Linos, earliest venturing music pierced numb barrenness; and in the shocked space whence a youth who was almost god-like had suddenly departed forever, emptiness first felt the vibration that now enchants and consoles and helps us?

—Rainer Maria Rilke

Faire is the Heaven
by William H. Harris

(text by Edmund Spenser)

Faire is the heav'n, where happy soules have place
In full enjoyment of felicitie;
Whence they doe still behold the glorious face
Of the Divine Eternall Majestie;
Yet farre more faire be those bright Cherubins
Which all with golden wings are overdight,
And those eternall burning Seraphins,
Which from their faces dart out fiery light;
Yet fairer than they both, and much more bright,
Be th' Angels and Archangels, which attend
On God's owne person, without rest or end.
These then in faire each other farre excelling,
As to that highest they approach more neare.
Yet is the highest farre beyond all telling,
Fairer than all the rest which their appear.
Though all their beauties joynd together were;
How then can mortall tongue hope to expresse
The image of such endless perfectnesse?

Eternitie from Seven Pious Pieces

by Donald Martino

(text by Robert Herrick)

O Yeares! and Age! Farewell:
Behold I go,
Where I do know
Infinitie to dwell.

And these mine eyes shall see
All times, how they
Are lost i' th' Sea
Of vast Eternitie.

Where never Moone shall sway
The Starres; but she
And Night,
shall be Drown'd
in one endless Day.

Allan Ramsay, *Sketch of a Dead Child*

VII

TRANSCENDENCE

Oh God, grant us a peaceful evening, a calm night, and a perfect end.

The Sleep

He giveth his beloved sleep –Ps. cxvii. 2.

Of all the thoughts of God that are
Borne inward unto souls afar,
Along the Psalmist's music deep,
Now tell me if that any is,
For gift or grace, surpassing this —
'He giveth His beloved sleep'?

What would we give to our beloved?
The hero's heart to be unmoved,
The poet's star-tuned harp, to sweep,
The patriot's voice, to teach and rouse,
The monarch's crown, to light the brows?
He giveth His beloved, sleep.

What do we give to our beloved?
A little faith all undisproved,
A little dust to overweep,
And bitter memories to make
The whole earth blasted for our sake.
He giveth His beloved, sleep.

'Sleep soft, beloved!' we sometimes say,
But have no tune to charm away
Sad dreams that through the eyelids creep.
But never doleful dream again
Shall break the happy slumber when
He giveth His beloved, sleep.

O earth, so full of dreary noises!
O men, with wailing in your voices!
O delved gold, the wailer's heap!
O strife, O curse, that o'er it fall!
God strikes a silence through you all,
He giveth His beloved, sleep.

His dews drop mutely on the hill;
His cloud above it saileth still,
Though on its slopes men sow and reap.
More softly that the dew is shed,
Or cloud is floated overhead,
He giveth His beloved, sleep.

Aye men may wonder while they scan
A living, thinking, feeling man
Confirmed in such a rest to keep;
But angels say, and through the word
I think their happy smile is heard—
He giveth His beloved, sleep.

For me, my heart that erst did go
Most like a child at a show,
That sees through tears the mummers leap,
Would now its wearied vision close,
Would child-like on His love repose,
Who giveth His beloved, sleep.

And, friends, dear friends, —when it shall be
That this low breath is gone from me,
And round my bier ye come to weep,
Let One, most loving of you all,
Say, 'Not a tear must o'er her fall;
He giveth His beloved, sleep.'

—Elizabeth Barrett Browning

Gustav Doré, *The Empyrean* (illustration from Dante's *Paradiso*)

Gottes Zeit ist die allerbeste Zeit BWV 106
by Johann Sebastian Bach

SONATINA

CHORUS

Of all times God's is the best.
In Him we live and move and have our being,
so long as he wills.
In Him we die at the appointed time,
when He wills.

ARIOSO—*tenor*

O Lord, teach us
to number our days,
that we may apply our hearts unto wisdom.

ARIA—*bass*

Set thine house in order,
for thou shalt die,
and not live.

CHORUS

The covenant from the beginning is,
Thou shalt die the death!

ARIOSO—*soprano* Even so, come, Lord Jesus.

ARIOSO—*countertenor* Into thy hands I commend my spirit,
for Thou hast redeemed me,
O Lord, thou God of truth.

ARIOSO—*bass* Today shalt thou be with me in paradise.

CHORALE With peace and joy do I depart
as God doth will;
my heart and mind are confident,
calm and tranquil,
as God did promise:
death is but as sleep to me.

CHORUS Glory, praise, honour and majesty
be with Thee, God the Father,
Son and Holy Ghost!
May God's power
lead us to victory
through Jesus Christ. Amen.

VOCES NOVAE

Aaron Kercheval, *Artistic Director*
Susan Swaney, *Music Director*
Carole A.C. Canfield
Chad Card
Sheila Carney
Andrew Cherry
Brian Cummings
Jason Damron
Robert Gehrenbeck
Christine Howlett
Aaron Kercheval
Kimberley A. Kercheval
Marvin Miller
Claudia Millicent
Marie Walker Monts
Alexandra Morphet
Alan Portzline
Hugh C. Resnick
Debra Shearer
Jill Suzanne Smith
Martin Duke Wilson

ADDITIONAL SINGERS

Charles Blandy
Cary Boyce
Michelle Boyle
Alexander deVaron
Andrew Hendricks
Ruth Kapustin
David McIntosh
Wendy Perrotta
Howard Swyers
Robert A. Taylor
Shari Woodbury

SOLOISTS

CARTER
Bridget Wintermann, *soprano*
BACH
Sumner Thompson, *bass*
Aaron Sheehan, *tenor*
Brian Cummings, *alto*

MUSICIANS

Leonard Hokanson, *piano*
Elżbieta Szmyt, *harp*

BARBER and MARTINO
Ruth Kapustin, *piano*
HAYDN
Roland Schwark, *cello*
HANDEL and MUSSARD
Grey Larsen, *flute*
MARAIS
August Denhard, *theorbo*
Kevin Lay, *viola da gamba*

LIAISON

Kevin Lay, *viola da gamba*
August Denhard, *theorbo*
Yonit Kosovske, *harpsichord*
WITH
Don Fader, *recorder*
Tricia van Oers, *recorder*

Mary Burke, *viola da gamba*
Roland Schwark, *cello*

READERS

Blythe Danner
Jennifer Harmon
Julie Harris
Edward Herrmann

IN MEMORY OF

John Babis

George G. Beanignet, Sr.

Eleanor A. Bucknam

Evelyn Cardew

Shirley Carpenter

Edna H. Cender

Patricia Dunlap

Alice Harmon

Reverend Larry Hill

Mary E. Jones

Florrie Keady

Christine Kercheval

Herb Kiesling

Harold H. Laird

Scott Marchant

Marshall and Emma May

Lillian E. McNulty

John Mendel

Richard and Sherlé Murdock

Mary Palmer

Kevin Pierce

Jean Portzline

Serena Portzline

James D. Ray, Jr.

Gabriel A. Sabga

Audrey Sewall

Rose Shainberg

Charles Shepherd

Otto Stahlke

W. Roy Stuemky

Vernater Taliaferro

Harry and Jennie Trubitt

Judith Vander Zee

Wayne H. Walker

Opal M. Wallace

THANKS TO

Sarah Ali · Cary Boyce · Craig Braun · Susan Piver Browne · Kara Hendricks ·
Jane Hill · Keith Jackson · Gesa Kordes · Jed Markson · Ed Maxedon · David McClees ·
Jim Olesen · Roy Renza · Lee Rhyne · Jeff Rothstein · Monica Shovlin · David Smith ·
Mary-Louise Smith · Ellen Surburg · Yvonne Thomas · Reverend John Vander Zee ·
Scott Weghorst · Michael Whitman

Choral pieces recorded in Recital Hall, Indiana University School of Music,
May 1999 and January 2000, David Meyer, Engineer.

Readings recorded at Star Trax, New York City, November 1999 and August 2000,
Roy Renza, Engineer; and Salisbury, Connecticut, February 2000.

Printing of CD books provided in part by Ivy Hill Corporation.
Replication of compact discs underwritten by Sony Corporation.

Provided with support from the Bloomington Area Arts Council, the Indiana Arts
Commission, a state agency, and the National Endowment for the Arts, a federal agency.

CITATIONS

Cover
& pg. xi
"Morning on the Seine near Giverny", Claude Monet, 1897. The Metropolitan Museum of Art, Bequest of Julia W. Emmons, 1956. (56.135.4) Copyright © 1996 by The Metropolitan Museum of Art.

pg. i
"The Angel of Death and the Sculptor from the Milmore Memorial", 1889-93, Daniel Chester French, 1926. The Metropolitan Museum of Art, Gift of a group of Museum trustees, 1926. (26.120) Photograph by Jerry L. Thompson. Copyright © 1998 by The Metropolitan Museum of Art.

pg. xiv
"Moonrise", Samuel Palmer, ©Leeds Museums and Galleries (City Art Gallery).

pg. 2
"Listening to Schumann"(En écoutant du Schumann), Fernand Khnopff, 1883. Musées royaux des Beaux-Arts de Belgique, Bruxells Koninklijke Musea voor Schone Kunsten van België, Brussel.

pg. 4
"TO MUSIC" for A Capella Chorus by Elliot Carter/Robert Herrick. Used by permission Peer International Corp.

pg. 5
"Sarabande", William Croft, Elżbieta Szmyt, harp. Copyright © 1995 Elżbieta Szmyt for Arch Music. Reproduced by permission of the artist.

pg. 6
"Ivy Branch", Henri Matisse, 1941, Art Gallery of Ontario, Toronto. Gift of Sam and Ayala Zacks, 1970. © 2000 Succession H. Matisse, Paris/Artists Rights Society (ARS), New York .

pg. 8
"The Open Window", Pierre Bonnard, 1921. The Phillips Collection, Washington, D.C. © 2000 Artists Rights Society (ARS), New York/ADAGP, Paris.

pg. 9
"i thank You God for most this amazing". Copyright 1950, © 1978, 1991 by the Trustees for the E.E. Cummings Trust. Copyright © 1979 by George James Firmage, from COMPLETE POEMS; 1904-1962 by E.E. Cummings, edited by George J. Firmage. Used by permission of Liveright Publishing Corporation.

pg. 10
"Sunday Morning" from COLLECTED POEMS by Wallace Stevens. Copyright

pg. 33   "Carols of Death", William Schuman, 1959, Merion Music, Inc./BMI.

pg. 36   "Dead Bird", Albert Pinkham Ryder, 1890's. The Phillips Collection, Washington, D.C.

pg. 37   "O Lord, Support Us", Calvin Hampton, 1975, McAfee Music Corporation.

pg. 38   "Acceptance" from THE POETRY OF ROBERT FROST edited by Edward Connery Lathem, © 1956 by Robert Frost, copyright 1928, 1969 by Henry Holt and Co. Reprinted by permission of Henry Holt and Company, LLC.

pg. 39   "e flat Intermezzo", Johannes Brahms, Leonard Hokanson, piano. Copyright © 1989 Bayer Records. Reproduced by permission of the artist.

pg. 41   Calyx-krater. Side A: Sleep and Death transporting the body of Sarpedon to Lycia, ca. 515 B.C. The Metropolitan Museum of Art, Purchase, Bequest of Joseph H. Durkee, Gift of Darius Ogden Mills and Gift of C. Ruxton Love, by exchange, 1972. (1972.11.10) Copyright © 1999 by The Metropolitan Museum of Art.

pg. 42   "Evocation", Pablo Picasso, 1901. © 2000 Estate of Pablo Picasso/Artists Rights Society (ARS), New York.

pg. 44   "The Voyage of Life: Old Age", Thomas Cole, 1840, Oil on canvas. Munson-Williams-Proctor Arts Institute, Museum of Art, Utica, New York, 55.108.

pg. 45   "Duino Elegy No. I", Rainer Maria Rilke. Source unknown.

pg. 50   "Faire is the Heaven", William H. Harris, 1925, Chappell & Co.

pg. 51   "Eternitie" from "Seven Pious Pieces", Donald Martino. © 1974 by Ione Press, Inc.; assigned 1998 to Donald Martino.

pg. 52   "Sketch of a Dead Child", Allan Ramsay. The National Gallery of Scotland.

Cover image:
Claude Monet
Morning on the Seine Near Giverny
Courtesy of The Metropolitan Museum of Art

Reverse image:
Daniel Chester French
The Angel of Death and the Sculptor from the Milmore Memorial
Courtesy of The Metropolitan Museum of Art

Design by 27.12 Design Ltd., NYC
www.2712design.com

Published by Voces Novae, Inc.
Copyright Voces Novae, Inc. 2001
www.vocesnovae.org